Pebble® Plus

Media Literacy for Kids

Learning About
Media Literacy

by Martha E. H. Rustad

Consulting Editor: Gail Saunders-Smith, PhD

Consultant: JoAnne DeLurey Reed
Librarian and Teacher, Scroggins Elementary School
Houston, Texas

CAPSTONE PRESS
a capstone imprint

Pebble Plus is published by Capstone Press,
1710 Roe Crest Drive, North Mankato, Minnesota 56003
www.capstonepub.com

Library of Congress Cataloging-in-Publication Data
Rustad, Martha E. H. (Martha Elizabeth Hillman), 1975–
  Learning about media literacy / by Martha E.H. Rustad.
      pages cm.—(Pebble plus. Media literacy for kids)
  Includes bibliographical references and index.
    ISBN 978-1-4914-1833-8 (library binding)—ISBN 978-1-4914-1838-3 (ebook)
1. Media literacy—Juvenile literature. I. Title.
  P96.M4R87 2015
  302.23—dc23   2014023678

Editorial Credits
Erika L. Shores, editor; Sarah Bennett, designer; Gene Bentdahl, production specialist

Photo Credits
Capstone Studio: Karon Dubke, 5, 9, 11, 13, 15, 17, 19, 21, cover; Shutterstock: Africa
Studio, 22, antb, 7, Tungphoto, 5 (TV)

Note to Parents and Teachers

The Media Literacy for Kids set supports Common Core State
Standards related to language arts. This book describes and illustrates
media. The images support early readers in understanding the text.
The repetition of words and phrases helps early readers learn new
words. This book also introduces early readers to subject-specific
vocabulary words, which are defined in the Glossary section. Early
readers may need assistance to read some words and to use the Table
of Contents, Glossary, Read More, Internet Sites, Critical Thinking
Using the Common Core, and Index sections of the book.

Printed in the United States of America in Stevens Point, Wisconsin.
092014   008479WZS15

Table of Contents

All About Media

We see and use media every day. Books, TV shows, and video games are media. Newspapers, the radio, and the Internet also are media.

Media tells or shows a message.
People use words, pictures,
and sounds to tell their ideas.
Computers and cameras are
used too.

7

Media literacy means understanding books, ads, shows, or stories. We understand who made the media and why.

First Space Stations

cross the globe hailed the Apollo
Yet most realized it was only
in the great journey into space.
ricans, Soviets, and others went
with the next steps. One was to
ate space stations in Earth orbit.
Astronauts and scientists

world live and work in these stations.
They would stay for weeks or even months.
The goal was to learn how to live in space
for extended periods. This was necessary
to future steps, such as creating industries
in space. Another planned step is to build
colonies on the moon and Mars.

Building orbiting space stations began
in 1971. The Soviets put the first space lab,
Salyut 1, into orbit. It circled Earth at a
height of 186 miles (300 km). The Americans
created their own station, Skylab, in 1973.
It orbited at 270 miles (435 km). The Skylab
crew carried out many studies. Some
looked at how long periods in space
the human body. They also took ph
of Earth. Some of these studies b
our knowledge of weather pat
showed forest growth and i

The U.S. Skylab I space
station orbiting high ab
the ground in 1974

THEN AND NOW: PET NAMES

Pet

From Racco
mascots ha

Mascots in all Mankato area schools are ani
with two exceptions: Loyola Catholic Sch
students are Crusaders; Mankato West stud
are the Scarlets.

Neither is an animal, though a big red bear lu
mysteriously in the history of Mankato High School, a
now, Mankato West.

On a Facebook page called "Mankato Memorie
several former students recall a fluffy, white teddy be
mascot, or a large, red bear as the mascot. Wrote Ga
Dubke, "Mike Lagow was the last person to my knowledg
to wear the 'bear' costume and assist the cheerleader
during football and basketball games. That was in 1975
76."

Although never official, Kay Menton recalls another
lled to service for the school, writing "Yeah it
ear but in other things they would use a red
panther for printing things up."

Free Press summer
essay series continues

Every Sunday this summer,
Free Press staff will be writing essays about what summer
memories and traditions they
and their families hold dear.
Features Editor Robb Murray
continues the series today. Look
for forthcoming essays right
here in the Currents section.

toward th
felt when all that
hanging out with my budui
Summers were sacred. We spent a
snowy school year yearning for their return,
and when they came, they raced by quicker
than a Chris Fairbanks fastball (which I
rarely ever caught up with, even on my best
day.) When we
weren't on the
ball field, we were
at my family's
cabin in northern
Wisconsin, or at
the playground
looking for a
pickup game, or, in
mid-teen years,

The Maker of the Message

Who are the people making media? Authors write stories. Artists make pictures and music. Designers design games.

The Audience

People write messages
for an audience.
The audience is anyone
who might see or hear
the media.

Elephants at Home
Rumble, rumble! The savanna ground shakes. A herd of elephants thunders by.
Elephants make their homes in many African habitats. They travel from savannas to forests to mountains. They ramble from deserts to swamps.
Design: Range Map
Just keep walking! Elephants migrate across Africa. Strong, solid legs carry their heavy gray bodies. They look for food and water.
acer
MacBook Air

A website for kids tells

about elephants.

Lucy finds the website.

She reads about

African elephants.

Information and Attention

Information might be missing from the message. The website has no facts on Asian elephants. Lucy will need more sources.

Elephants Are Mammals

Elephants are mammals. Mammals are warm-blooded animals. Female elephants feed milk to their young. Elephants have a backbone. Elephants are the largest mammals that live on land.

FUN FACT

Asian elephants have ears that are three times smaller than African elephants' ears.

Asian elephants

Media makers want their audiences to pay attention. The elephant website has pictures and fun songs. Kids like using that site.

Creating Media

We read, listen to, and watch media. We also write and draw media. What message will you tell today?

Activity: Puppet Show

Work with your class or a group of friends to make a puppet show. Talk about the kinds of media you will use to make your show. Talk about how a puppet show is also a kind of media. What is the message of your puppet show?

1. Choose your story. Act out part of a favorite book or movie. Or write your own story.

2. Design puppets. Draw and cut out the characters. Glue them to craft sticks. Or make puppets from old socks.

3. Make a stage. Put a blanket over a table. Hide behind the table. Reach your puppets above the table.

4. Practice your puppet show. When you are ready, perform for your friends. Or ask an adult to record your show.

What You Need

paper

crayons

craft sticks

old socks

blanket

table

Glossary

ad—a notice that calls attention to a product or an event; ad is short for advertisement

artist—a person who draws or makes art

audience—people who hear, read, or see a message

author—a person who writes a book, website, or script

designer—a person who makes a video game or an online game

media—a way to tell or show a message; books, movies, TV shows, advertisements, games, websites, and music are all kinds of media

Read More

Gaines, Ann Graham. *Master the Library and Media Center.* Ace It! Information Literacy Series. Berkeley Heights, N.J.: Enslow Publishers, 2009.

Kaplan, Arie. *The Awesome Inner Workings of Video Games.* Shockzone: Games and Gamers. Minneapolis: Lerner Publications Company, 2014.

Rustad, Martha E. H. *How Books Are Made.* Wonderful World of Reading. North Mankato, Minn.: Capstone Press, 2013.

Internet Sites

FactHound offers a safe, fun way to find Internet sites related to this book. All of the sites on FactHound have been researched by our staff.

Here's all you do:

Visit *www.facthound.com*

Type in this code: 9781491418338

Critical Thinking Using the Common Core

Describe one or two ways media makers grab the attention of an audience. (Key Ideas and Details)

Why is it important to know who made the media and who their audience is? (Integration of Knowledge and Ideas)

Index

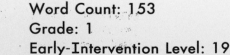
Word Count: 153
Grade: 1
Early-Intervention Level: 19